Greatest
Stories
from the
QURAN

Also by the same author

Tell Me About the Prophet Muhammad
Tell Me About Hajj
Tell Me About the Prophet Musa
Tell Me About the Prophet Yusuf
Quran Stories for Kids
The Junior Encyclopaedia of Islam
I'm Learning About Eid-ul-Fitr
I'm Learning About the Prophet Muhammad
The Honoured Guests
The Light of Allah
Luqman's Advise to His Son
The Morals of Believers
The Story of Two Gardens
The Treasure House
The Uzayr's Donkey
The Wise Man and the Prophet Musa
Nursed in the Desert
A Visit to Madinah
The Search for Truth
I See Allah Everywhere
The Spider's House
The Story of the Fly

Goodword Books Pvt. Ltd.
1, Nizamuddin West Market, New Delhi - 110 013
E-mail: info@goodwordbooks.com
Printed in India
Illustrated by Pulak Biswas
© Goodword Books 2007
First published 2002
Reprinted 2007
www.goodwordbooks.com

The
Greatest
Stories
from the
QURAN

S A N I Y A S N A I N   K H A N

Goodwordkidz
Helping you build a family of faith

Contents

In the Beginning

Allah said the word, "Be" and by
His just saying it, the earth and the sky
came into existence. Allah made
the earth in two days. One day of Allah
is equal to one thousand years
by our reckoning.

Allah made two great lights for the world—the sun to shine like gold by day and the moon to shine like silver by night. Allah also made the stars twinkle and shine. Then came the dry land and the oceans. By just saying the words, Allah made them all.

The Garden of Paradise

Allah created the first man from earth and named him Adam.

Allah also created the first woman, Hawwa (Eve), as a helper and loving companion of Adam ﷺ.
Allah told them to live in the garden of Paradise, but warned them not to approach a particular tree.
However, Satan whispered to them, tempting them to approach the forbidden tree. So they ate from the tree and became wrongdoers. But no sooner had they done so, than they realized their fault, and feeling very sorry, they turned to Allah. Allah forgave them both, but told them to leave the gardens of Paradise and go down to earth.

Allah told them that from time to time His messengers and prophets would be coming to the earth to guide the people to the true path. Those who followed His commands and lived a righteous life would have no fear of Judgement Day and would be admitted to Paradise. But those who disbelieved and rejected Allah's signs would be taken to task and thrown into the fire of Hell.

The Sacrifice of the Brothers

The Prophet Adam ﷺ and Hawwa had two sons, Habil (Abel) who became a shepherd, and Qabil (Cain) who worked as a farmer.

One day the two sons decided to make a sacrifice to Allah. Habil offered the best of his flock, while Qabil offered his crops.

Suddenly a bolt of lightning burnt Habil's offering to ashes, showing that Allah accepted his sacrifice, but not Qabil's.

This made Qabil hate and envy his younger brother.

Habil explained that Qabil's sacrifice had been rejected because he did not fear Allah. But Qabil, feeling disgraced and insulted, cried, "No, I will kill you!" Habil merely said that even if he tried to do so, he would not fight back, because he feared "Allah, the Lord of the Worlds".

But in a rage, Qabil killed his innocent brother Habil.

This story tells us that believers should never fight, and even if one raises his hand, the other should never strike back.

The Quran says : "If anyone killed a person—except as punishment for murder or other corruption in the land—it shall be looked upon as if he had killed all mankind. And whoever saved a human life, shall be looked upon as if he had saved all mankind."
(*Surah al-Maidah*, 5:32)

The Ark of the Prophet Nuh ﷺ

Men and women had children and then there were families. But soon the Children of Adam ﷺ began to worship idols. This custom displeased Allah, so he sent the Prophet Nuh (Noah) ﷺ to his erring people to guide them to the right path.

Nuh ﷺ went to his people to give them the message of Allah. He spoke to them in public, and preached to them in private. After years of hardship and struggle, only a handful of poor people listened to his call.

Each time he urged them to ask for Allah's pardon, they would thrust their fingers in their ears, and draw their cloaks over their heads. At last Nuh ﷺ warned his people of an approaching flood, hoping that that would persuade them to win Allah's favor. He pointed to the many holes in the earth which were filling up with water and showed them how the rivers were overflowing their banks.
But his people only laughed at him and said: "Bring down the punishment you threaten, if what you say be true."

The people turned against him and tried to kill him.
In great distress, Nuh ﷺ prayed to his Lord:
"Help me Lord, I am overcome."

The Great Flood

Later Allah revealed to the Prophet Nuh ﷺ that now none of his people would believe in him, except those who had already shown their trust in him, and that He had decided to send a terrible flood which would destroy everyone but Nuh ﷺ and his followers. Allah then ordered him to "build an Ark under Our watchful eyes."

After a very long period of hard, tiring work, the Ark was finally ready. Then Nuh ﷺ said: "Embark! In the name of Allah, it shall set sail and cast anchor. My Lord is forgiving and merciful." Allah then asked Nuh ﷺ to take aboard with him a pair of every living creature along with his faithful believers.

No sooner had they all come on board, than the rain
began to fall. More and more rain fell each day.
The rivers overflowed and water fell in torrents.

The Ark rose and fell on mountainous waves but when the
flood had reached its peak, Allah commanded the sky to
hold back the rain. The clouds began to part and the rain
stopped and, as the level of the water began to go down,
the mountain peaks began to reappear. The Ark came to
rest on Mount Judi, in a land now known as Turkey.

The Prophet Nuh عليه السلام and his companions thanked
Allah for saving them from such a devastating flood.
Everyone happily came out of the Ark. The animals
were led to safety.

Nuh عليه السلام prayed: "Lord, let my landing from this Ark be
blessed, for You alone can make me land in safety."

Allah's Best Friend

Long, long ago, about 4000 years ago, in the faraway land of Iraq, a boy named Ibrahim (or Abraham) ﷺ was born in the village of Ur. He was so gracious, tender-hearted and pure in faith that Allah gave him wisdom when he was still a child, and made him His best friend.

In those days, people used to worship stones and statues, but even as a child Ibrahim ﷺ wondered why. Once when the townspeople were away, he broke all the idols in the temple, except the biggest. When asked who has done this. Ibrahim ﷺ calmly replied, "Ask the biggest idol. Why do you worship things that cannot even talk, move or understand?" They became furious, and tried to kill him, by burning him alive.

But Allah was with him. Allah commanded the fire, "O fire, be cool and peaceful for Ibrahim." A miracle took place, and the fire, instead of burning Ibrahim ﷺ, became a cool refuge for him.

The moral of the story is that faith in Allah is the only thing that can save a believer in this world and the world to come.

The Lonely, Barren Valley

When Ibrahim ﷺ grew up, he became a great prophet, and preached Allah's message first in his own land, then later in Syria, Palestine and Egypt.

When a beautiful son was born to his wife, Hajar (or Hagar), Allah ordered Ibrahim ﷺ to take the mother and baby Ismail (Ishmael) ﷺ to the place now known as Makkah. It took them a long time to reach the lonely, barren valley, near two small hills called Safa and Marwah. Ibrahim ﷺ, ordered by Allah to leave his baby there along with his wife, then departed. Little Ismail ﷺ soon began to cry for water. Hajar ran from one hill to another, but there was not a drop of water to drink, nor was there any human being to give her any.

Allah then mercifully performed a miracle—a spring (later known as Zamzam) gushed forth beneath the baby's feet. Hajar then gave some fresh spring water to the thirsty child, and so his life was saved. Ismail ﷷ and his mother began to live in the valley and, because of the Zamzam spring, more people gradually settled there, slowly building up a small town, later called Makkah.

The moral of the story is that believers who, despite their hardships, follow the path of Allah, will find that Allah will help them in miraculous ways, just as the child Ismail ﷷ was saved by the miracle of the Zamzam spring.

The Great Sacrifice

One night, the Prophet Ibrahim ﷺ dreamt that, to please his Lord, he was sacrificing his son, Ismail ﷺ. Ismail ﷺ was still a child, but he was a brave boy and when told about the dream he was quite ready to obey Allah's command. Without hesitating, he said, "Do what you are commanded father: God willing, you will find me one of the steadfast."

Ibrahim ﷺ then took his son to a place, now known as Mina—a valley near Makkah. Satan appeared there and tried to dissuade him from sacrificing his son but Ibrahim ﷺ just pelted him with pebbles.

As Ibrahim ﷺ took up a knife to sacrifice Ismail ﷺ, Allah sent the angel Jibril (Gabriel) with a ram to be sacrificed instead.

Allah was so pleased with the readiness of the Prophet Ibrahim ﷺ to sacrifice his beloved son, that He commanded the believers to observe this day as Id al-Adha or the Feast of Sacrifice.

The First Call for Hajj

Ismail ﷺ grew up a strong and loving youth. The Prophets Ibrahim ﷺ and Ismail ﷺ were ordered by Allah to build the House of God—the Kabah in Makkah. They took stones from the nearby hills and started to work.

As the Prophets Ibrahim ﷺ and Ismail ﷺ laid the very first stones, they prayed, "Our Lord, accept this from us! You are the All-hearing, the All-seeing." They further prayed, "Our Lord, make us bow to You, and make our offspring a nation which bows to You and show us our ways of worship." The Prophet Ibrahim ﷺ was ordered by Allah to clean the Kabah for those who came there to pray, and to call people to Hajj: "Call all people to make the Pilgrimage. They shall come to you on foot and on the backs of swift camels; they shall come from every deep ravine." And so Allah made it a duty for all Muslims, male and female, to go on Hajj once in a lifetime, provided their means and health permitted.

The Pious Man and His Sons

The Prophet Yaqub, or Jacob, was a pious man. He lived in Canaan, some thirty miles north of Jerusalem. He and his family lived in tents. He had twelve sons. Yusuf ﷷ was the second youngest of them.

One day, Yusuf had an unusual dream, in which eleven stars and the sun and the moon all bowed down to him. When his father heard about this dream, he understood that great things lay in store for his young and best-loved son. For their part, being aware of

their father's love for Yusuf ﷺ, the ten big brothers became so resentful that they began to hate him. They would go off to look after the family's flocks, grumbling and muttering.
They became so jealous of their father's love for this younger brother that they banded together and hatched a plot to kill him.

One day they took him with them pretending that they were going out for a picnic. Coming close to a well, they took him unaware, and seizing him from behind, they dragged him to the well and threw him down into it. He screamed as he fell, but they paid no heed. The well was deep, but it was dried up. Yusuf ﷺ landed on the dry bottom of the well with a thud. There would be no climbing those slippery sides to escape. But he was a brave boy, and did not cry. His courage never failed him. He turned towards his Lord for help.

Sweet Patience

While his dear father sorrowed for him, Yusuf ﷺ lay at the bottom of the dark well for about three nights. In the meanwhile, a caravan from Syria heading for Egypt camped near the well. One of the caravan people threw his bucket into the well to fetch some water. But, to his surprise, when he pulled up his bucket, there was a good looking boy clinging to it. The caravan people took him to Egypt and sold him to an Egyptian prince, who was called the Aziz. The Aziz took this innocent and good natured boy to his wife and told her to take good care of him.

The years passed and Yusuf ﷺ grew into a young man of remarkable beauty and charm. The Aziz's wife, whose name was Zulaykha, felt very attracted to Yusuf ﷺ, but he kept his distance and never responded to her advances. Zulaykha threatened to have him sent to prison. In great anguish, Yusuf ﷺ prayed: "O Lord, prison will be better than what I am being asked to do."

But, even although Yusuf ﷺ was innocent, Zulaykha decided to imprison him.

Prison opens another chapter in the life of the Prophet Yusuf ﷺ. Here he met two prisoners. They were servants in the royal court, who had displeased the king. Both of them had strange dreams, the meanings of which were correctly given by Yusuf ﷺ. One of them, a cup bearer, was freed and taken back into the king's service.

One day the king dreamt that seven lean cows were eating up seven fat ones and seven green ears of corn were being replaced by seven dried up ones. No one was able to say what this unusual dream meant. At that time, at the

request of the cup bearer, Yusuf ﷺ interpreted the dream. He explained that in the lands of Egypt there would be seven years of prosperity. But following these seven years of abundance, there would come seven years of dreadful famine.

The king greatly liked his explanation. There and then he appointed him to look after the granaries and charged him with providing enough grain to meet all needs during the foretold famine seven years later. Yusuf ﷺ had become the most trusted minister of the King of Egypt.

The Family Unites

The seven good years passed and then, as foretold by Yusuf عَلَيْهِ السَّلَام, there came the seven lean and hungry years, when no crops would grow and famine held the land in its grip. Back in the land of Canaan, Yaqub عَلَيْهِ السَّلَام and his sons were hit by the famine too. Therefore, the ten sons travelled to Egypt in search of grain.

When they came to the chief of the store houses in Egypt, Yusuf عَلَيْهِ السَّلَام recognized them, but little did they know that this minister, from whom they had come to seek provisions, was their own brother Yusuf whom they had thrown into a dry well many years before.

Yusuf ﷻ received them honorably, and asked them about their family. Yusuf ﷻ gave them an ample supply of grain and put their money back in their packs. The brothers made further visits, then, ultimately Yusuf ﷻ revealed his identity to them and forgave them for their crime. He asked them to bring their aged parents. Finally the family was reunited and Yusuf ﷻ embraced his parents and did them honor by making them sit on the throne, saying: "Welcome to Egypt, in safety if Allah will!" Seeing the splendor and high position of Yusuf ﷻ, they all fell prostrate, as a mark of thanksgiving and awe. "This," Yusuf ﷻ reminded his father, "is the meaning of my dream, which my Lord has fulfilled." The dream that Yusuf ﷻ had as a boy, of the sun, the moon and the eleven stars prostrating themselves before him, had at last come true.

The Queen Who Saved the Baby

About 3000 years ago, Egypt was ruled by a very cruel king called Firawn or Pharaoh.

One day a court soothsayer told Firawn that that year a boy would be born among the tribe of the Banu Israil (or the Children of Israel) who would destroy him and his kingdom. Enraged, Firawn ordered all newborn boys of the tribe to be killed. The Banu Israil, already enslaved by Firawn, suffered the torment of seeing their newborn sons killed, while only their daughters were spared. During these horrible times a pious woman, called Yukabid, of the Banu Israil, gave birth to a beautiful boy who was named Musa, or Moses. She was told by Allah that this was a very special child who would one day become a great prophet.

Allah inspired her to put him in a box, which she was to cast into the river Nile, with the promise that her baby would be safe. She obeyed Allah's order, and as the waves carried the box away, his sister kept a watch on it, until it stopped at a bank near the royal palace. There it was picked up by a member of Firawn's household and brought to the queen. The queen was a loving, kind-hearted woman. When she saw the baby, her heart was touched and she exclaimed:

"What a lovely child! Whoever sees him cannot but love him."

Despite the king's objection, the queen decided to keep the baby in the palace and rear him as her own child.

Allah Speaks to Musa علیهِ السلام

The Prophet Musa علیهِ السلام, brought up with loving care by the Queen, received the best education.

But because Musa علیهِ السلام accidentally killed someone, Firawn intended to slay him. Therefore, Musa علیهِ السلام quietly left the city and journeyed to Madyan, where he met the Prophet Shuyab and married his daughter. After spending some years in the beautiful valley of Madyan, Musa علیهِ السلام returned with his family to Egypt.
They travelled slowly towards Mount Sinai, passing through awesome landscapes of desert and rock.
One cold winter evening, as it grew darker and a cool breeze began to blow, they seemed to have lost their way.
Musa علیهِ السلام looked around and noticed a fire quite far away on the side of a mountain. He said: "Wait here!
Look, I can see a fire in the distance. Perhaps I can find out where we are, or at least get a burning brand to warm ourselves with!"

As Musa علیهِ السلام reached the source of the light, Allah spoke to him and gave him wisdom and miracles. Allah told him that He had chosen him as His messenger and commanded him to go with these signs and give His message to Firawn, who had made himself a tyrant in the land.

The King's Magicians

Inspired by Allah and armed with His clear signs, Musa ﷺ reached the court of Firawn along with his brother Harun ﷺ. But Firawn rejected them outright. To convince him, Musa ﷺ threw down his staff, and it turned into a huge snake. Then he drew out his hand from his armpit, and it was shining brightly. But Firawn rejected these miracles, calling them magic.

Firawn called his best magicians to outdo the Prophet Musa ﷺ. The magicians threw down their magic ropes and sticks. These now looked like live snakes and serpents writhing on the ground. Musa ﷺ was horrified, as the snakes seemed to coil and uncoil around him.

As Musa ﷺ threw down his staff, all of a sudden it became a huge snake. What was more amazing was that it began to eat up all the other snakes one after another, until it had eaten them all up. Everyone was wonderstruck. The magicians fell on the ground in adoration, exclaiming, "We believe in the Lord of Musa and Harun."

But Firawn, raged violently and growing more and more stubborn, punished the magicians.
He soon redoubled his torment of the Banu Israil tribe.

The Cruel King Drowned

Faced with Firawn's worst cruelty, the Prophet Musa ﷺ was finally commanded by Allah to leave Egypt along with the entire tribe of the Banu Israil. Therefore, one night, fearing Firawn's wrath, Musa ﷺ and his followers secretly departed. When Firawn was informed about this, he set out with his huge army with its many chariots, horsemen and soldiers to punish the Banu Israil.

Musa ﷺ and his followers, marching ahead, were about to reach the sea, when some of them spotted a great cloud of dust to their rear. This struck great terror into the entire caravan, as they realized that Firawn's great army was pursuing them. As Firawn's troops drew nearer, hemming them in, Allah told Musa ﷺ to strike the sea with his staff.

No sooner had Musa ﷺ done so, than a great miracle took place. The waves of the sea began to split into two halves. A path across the sea had opened up and Musa ﷺ and his people thanked Allah as they safely crossed over.

Musa ﷺ and his followers were barely across when Firawn and his army arrived at the banks of the sea. Unmoved by Allah's miracle, Firawn decided to go on pursuing Musa ﷺ. But when Firawn and his army were halfway across, the waves, standing obediently on either side like huge walls, turned back into water and fell on them. Firawn and all his army were instantly crushed and drowned. Once across, Musa ﷺ and all his followers landed safely in the Sinai Peninsula. The Prophet Musa ﷺ called on his people to remember Allah's goodness in saving them from Firawn and to be thankful to Him for His favor.

The Prophet King

Many many years after the death of the Prophet Musa ﷺ in the eleventh century B.C., there was much unrest among the Banu Israil due to several invasions of their homeland. During a battle Dawud (David) ﷺ, who was still in his youth fought and killed Jalut (Goliath), a giant commander of the enemy. For this reason, Dawud ﷺ was made the king.

He was granted prophethood at the age of forty and Zabur (the Psalms) were revealed to him.

Dawud was also taught the language of the birds. When he recited the Zabur, the birds would also join him in praising Allah. The mountains too used to praise Allah along with him. He was given special help against his enemies, and the wisdom to judge between the Truth and falsehood.

The Valley of Ants

The Prophet Sulayman (Solomon) عليه السلام was the son of the Prophet Dawud (David) عليه السلام. Dawud عليه السلام was a mighty king and ruled Jerusalem. He was given wonderful powers by Allah.

When Sulayman عليه السلام grew up, he was blessed with prophethood and was also made king. Allah gave him special knowledge. He was able to understand the language of the birds. By Allah's special favor, he could control the winds. He was also in control of the jinn. He used to employ them in whatever way he liked.

One day Sulayman ﷺ was passing through a valley at the head of his mighty army. In this valley there lived a large number of ants. Seeing the huge army coming, one of the ants loudly and hurriedly warned its fellow ants: "O you ants, run off home before Sulayman and his army tread on you by mistake!" Because of Allah's great mercy to Sulayman ﷺ, he was able to understand languages that others could not. So he heard the ant's plea and smiled. Then he was suddenly startled by the thought of how merciful Allah had been to him. He turned to his Lord in praise and prayed:

"O my Lord! Make me grateful to You for Your favors,
which You have given me and my parents,
and I will do what is right to please You.
And by Your grace, make me one of
Your righteous servants."

The Queen and the Bird

One day, the hudhud (hoopoe) said to Sulayman ﷺ (who understood the language of the birds): "I have just seen something you know nothing of. I come to you from faraway Sheba, where I found a woman ruler. She is blessed with every virtue and has a splendid throne. But she and her subjects worship the sun instead of Allah." With this the hudhud praised Allah: "There is no deity save Allah! He is Lord of the Supreme Throne!"

Sulayman ﷺ then had one of his aides, who was deeply versed in the Book, bring her throne to him in the twinkling of an eye. Seeing the glittering throne, Sulayman ﷺ displayed no pride but humbly prostrated himself in gratitude to Allah: "This is a favor from my Lord to test my gratitude. He who gives thanks has much to gain; but he who is ungrateful will surely lose. As for Allah, He has no needs. He is supreme in Honor!" When the Queen reached Jerusalem, she was invited to sit on the throne, which had been slightly altered. She realized, however, that it was her own throne, and was amazed at the power of Allah.

Sulayman ﷺ ushered her into his beautiful palace.
When she stepped on to the floor, she tucked up her skirts,
thinking it was a pool of water.

But Sulayman ﷺ explained that it was just a floor of glass beneath which water flowed. It looked like something which it was not. In the same way, there was only one reality, and that was Allah—the Creator. Everything was His creation. So the Queen should give up worshipping the sun and worship the Creator of all things. She understood the Prophet Sulayman's words and at once accepted his message, saying: "O my Lord, I have indeed sinned, I now submit (in Islam), with Sulayman, to the Lord of the World."

The Most Honorable Woman

About 700 years before the birth of the Prophet Muhammad ﷺ, there lived in Jerusalem a pious woman called Hannah (Anne). Her husband was Imran. Hannah prayed to Allah for a child and vowed that the child would be devoted to His service. Allah heard her prayers, and she gave birth to a beautiful baby girl who was named Maryam (Mary). But Hannah was disappointed, for traditionally, only a male child could do priestly work. But Allah graciously accepted her and caused her to grow up in purity.

When Maryam was dedicated to the service of Allah, the priests were so impressed by her devoutness that every one of them felt it would be an honor to take her under his wing.

To decide who her guardian should be, they drew lots, but each time, they were in favor of the Prophet Zakariyya ﷺ, who was Maryam's uncle and also the chief priest at the Temple in Jerusalem. So she grew up under his loving care.

Whenever Zakariyya ﷺ went to see Maryam praying in the prayer-niche, he would find fresh food and would ask in amazement: "O Maryam! Where is this food from?" "From Allah," she would answer. "Allah gives without measure to whom He pleases."

Thus Maryam was raised to be a pious and most devout servant of Allah. Soon she became known for her purity, serenity and very great virtue.

Food From the Heavens

One day when Maryam was praying alone in her prayer-niche, Allah sent an angel to her in human form. Taken aback she said, "May the Merciful defend me from you! If you fear the Lord, leave me alone and go your way." "I am the messenger of your Lord," replied the angel, "and have come to announce the gift of a holy son."

Maryam later gave birth to a son whom Allah had already named Isa ibn Maryam (Jesus, son of Mary). When she returned with the baby, fingers were pointed at her, but she simply pointed to the baby who performed his first miracle, by saying at once:

"I am the servant of Allah. He has given me the Book and made me a prophet. His blessing is upon me wherever I go, and He has commanded me to be steadfast in prayer and give alms to the poor as long as I shall live. He has made me kind and dutiful towards my mother. He has rid me of arrogance and wickedness. I was blessed on the day I was born,

and blessed I shall be on the day of my death; and may peace be upon me on the day when I shall be raised to life."

He was also given the power to perform a number of miracles, such as moulding a bird out of clay, which, when he breathed on it, came to life. He gave sight to the blind, cured lepers and even raised the dead to life. But despite these clear signs, the people of Israel rejected him, accusing him of sorcery. Only a handful of his disciples responded to his call, saying, "We are the helpers of Allah."

One day the disciples asked him whether his Lord could send down a table spread with food from the heavens. "Fear Allah," warned Isa ﷺ, "if you are true believers." But they insisted and in answer to the Prophet Isa's prayer, angels brought down a table spread with delicious food—a unique miracle.

'Isa ﷺ continued his mission for several years, but only a few answered his call. The Banu Israil wanted to crucify him. But Allah saved him and they crucified another man, who was made to appear like him.

Sleepers in the Cave

It was about A.D. 250, during the rule of the Roman King Decius (Daqyanus) that seven young men of a noble family accepted the teachings of the Prophet Isa ﷺ. But King Decius took up arms against them. When they realized that the king's soldiers were about to capture them, these young believers ran away from the town to take refuge in a dark cave. There they prayed to Allah: "Our Lord! Bestow Your Mercy on us and save our lives." Allah heard their prayers and, when they lay down to rest, He made them fall into a deep sleep lasting 200 years. Not once during this time did they awaken.

With the passage of time the town they left had changed altogether. The cruel king had died and the present king became a believer, a follower of the message of the Prophet Isa ﷺ. During this period, Allah woke up the sleeping men. When the new king came to know about them, he himself came on foot to see them and seek their blessings. When these young men died, a shrine was built at their cave as a memorial.

The story tells us that those who put their entire trust in Allah, will be helped by Him from unknown sources.

The Iron Wall

Long, long ago, during the sixth century B.C.
King Dhul Qarnayn ruled the lands from the Aegean Sea to
the Indus River. He was just and righteous, protecting
the weak and punishing the law-breakers.

When he tooks his armies to the North East of Iran,
he reached the Caucasus mountain range which runs
between the Caspian and the Black Seas. Once, in that
region, he met a tribe who begged him to protect them from
the wild tribes, the Yajuj and the Majuj (Gog and Magog)
who kept coming through the mountain passes, and
attacking them.

Dhul Qarnayan asked for iron blocks and molten brass and, with the help of the local people, he built a barrier across the valley to hold back the Yajuj and Majuj.

After conquering a major part of the then inhabited world Dhul Qarnayan had lost none of his humility. He gave the entire credit for his feats to the blessing of Allah. Of the iron wall he had built, he said:

"This is a blessing from my Lord. But when my Lord's promise has been fulfilled, He will level it to dust. And the promise of my Lord is true."

Tale of A Fish

A very old and powerful community used to live around 800 B.C., in Nineveh, some 230 miles north west of Baghdad. Allah sent the Prophet Yunus (Jonah) ﷺ to this community to guide them on to the right path.

Yunus ﷺ preached to them for a long time, warning them to turn away from their wickedness, but they paid no heed to his words. Angry and despairing, Yunus ﷺ left these people, and headed towards the seaport where he boarded a ship. No sooner was it asail than the sky grew dark, and there was a terrible storm, with huge waves crashing against the ship's hull.

Thinking their ill-luck was due to some slave having run away, the sailors drew lots to find the man and hurl him overboard. The name of Yunus ﷺ was picked out in the draw. So he was forced to jump from the ship. As he struggled in the water, gasping for breath, a great whale appeared out of the depths of the sea and swallowed him up. Suddenly Yunus ﷺ found himself in the dark, damp insides of the huge fish. He had not drowned. He was still alive! Now Yunus ﷺ realized that he had left the people of Nineveh too early without completing the task set by Allah.

When Yunus ﷺ realized his mistake, he cried from the depths of darkness: "There is no god but You. Glory be to You! I have done wrong." Allah heard his prayers. The fish, at Allah's behest, swam close to the land and left Yunus ﷺ safely on the beach, where he found himself under a tree. Yunus ﷺ then returned to his people and preached to them again. All of them, over one hundred thousand, responded to his call.

The Story of Two Gardens

Long, long ago, there lived two friends, one a rich gardener, and the other a poor farmer. The gardener owned a huge plot of land, which he very ably turned into two beautiful, well-watered gardens full of flowers and all kind of fruits, especially grapes and dates. He thought all this was the result of his hard work and clever planning, rather than a blessing from Allah, without whose help nothing can be achieved on this earth.

One day he showed the poor farmer around his garden and proudly said to him, "I am richer than you and my clan is mightier than yours. And surely this will never perish! Nor do I believe that the hour of Doom will ever come." Then he added: "Even if I return to my Lord, I shall surely find a better place than this." But all this was just wishful thinking.

When the poor farmer saw his friend behave in this wicked way, he asked: "Have you no faith in Him who created you from dust, from a little germ, and fashioned you into a man? As for myself, Allah is my Lord, and I will associate no one else with Him. Instead of entering the garden proudly, you should have acted humbly and said: 'What Allah has ordained must surely come to pass: there is no strength except in Allah.'" Though I am poorer and have fewer children," the farmer argued, "my Lord may give me a garden better than yours, and blast your vineyards with thunderbolts or drain off their water so that you will get no benefit." The very next day calamity struck. The rich man's garden was laid waste. All the fruits were destroyed and the vines had tumbled down upon their trellises. Realising his mistake, he cried, "If only I had served no other gods besides my Lord!"

This story is meant to teach believers never to speak proudly, but to say in all humility, "Whatever Allah has ordained must surely come to pass: there is no power save with Allah."

The Camel and the Evil People

Salih ﷺ, a prophet born into the Thamud tribe, was sent to mankind in northern Arabia, after the Great Flood. Disappointed to see his people worshipping idols, he asked them to pray to Allah alone, saying: "Remember, He made you the heirs of Ad, and provided you with dwellings in the land. You have built mansions on its plains and hew out houses from the mountains. Remember Allah's favor and do not corrupt the earth with wickedness. Will you not fear Allah? I am indeed your true messenger. Fear Allah and follow me. For this I ask nothing in return; none can reward me except the Lord of the Universe. Are you to be left secure in this land, amidst gardens and fountains, cornfields and date-laden palm-trees, hewing your dwellings out of the mountains and leading a wanton life? Go in fear of Allah and follow me."

But the elders of the Thamud tribe, holding to their old religion, arrogantly scorned the idea of the Day of Judgement. They called Salih ﷺ a foolish liar and branded him and his followers as evil and not to be trusted.

Finally, to test them, Salih ﷺ entrusted Allah's own she-camel (*naqat Allah*), to their care. He threatened them with a scourge if they mistreated her. But they heedlessly had her slaughtered, then haughtily challenged Salih ﷺ, if he was really Allah's messenger, to bring down his scourge upon them. Salih ﷺ then told them they had only three days to live in their houses, before Allah's will was done. Even then, instead of repenting, they plotted to kill Salih ﷺ. But, before they could carry out their evil plot, Allah brought them all to ruin with a terrible earthquake.

The Most Patient Man

The Prophet Ayyub, or Job ﷺ, a great Prophet who lived in the ninth century B.C. in Hawran near Damascus in Syria, set great examples for mankind.

Apart from his great wisdom and compassion, Ayyub ﷺ was also a very rich man. He had huge herds of cattle, vast fields, a large family and many friends. Yet, he remained an extremely steadfast and sincere servant of Allah, and was forever calling others to worship Him. But Satan made people think that it was only because Ayyub ﷺ was wealthy that he lived a good life, and that if his blessings were taken away, he would no longer be grateful to Allah. To put him to the test, Allah struck him with a series of calamities. His cattle and crops were destroyed, his children died and, worst of all, he became very ill, remaining bedridden for many years. Within a very short

62

period of time, Ayyub ﷺ became very poor and his friends left him one by one. But Ayyub ﷺ was not angry. He put his entire trust in Allah, being confident that Allah knew everything. When his suffering and loneliness worsened and his sickness and pain became unbearable, Ayyub ﷺ turned to Allah in humble prayer, crying: "I am overcome by distress. But You are the most Merciful of those that are merciful."

Allah heard his beautiful prayer, and put an end to his long and terrible hardship. He ordered Ayyub ﷺ to strike the ground with his feet. He did as commanded, and by a miracle, a spring of fresh water gushed forth. No sooner did Ayyub ﷺ take a bath in it, than his illness was cured and he regained his former health and strength. Because Ayyub ﷺ showed great patience throughout the worst of disasters, Allah not only rewarded him with great bounty in the Hereafter, but redoubled his former prosperity in this world. He had a new family of seven sons and three daughters. He lived to the ripe old age of 93 and saw four generations. He became so rich that it was said that "he was rained upon with locusts of gold."

The Search for Truth

The Prophet Muhammad ﷺ was born in 570 AD in Makkah. When he grew up, a desire to know the truth began to grow in him. He would sit for hours in the solitude of nature up in the cave of Hira, near Makkah. He would pray and meditate, beseeching the Maker of the heavens and the earth for answers to the questions which were surging in his mind. What is man's true role in life? What does the Lord requires of us, as His servants? Where does man come from and where does he go after death?

One day, after many days of meditation, the Archangel Jibril appeared before Muhammad ﷺ in human form, and taught him these beautiful verses from the Quran:

Read: In the name of your Lord who created.
Created man from a clot.

Read: And your Lord is the Most
Generous Who taught by the pen.
Taught man what he knew not.

This was how the revelation of the Quran began. Not only did Allah grant him guidance, but He also chose Muhammad ﷺ as His last Prophet and special envoy to mankind.

The Quraysh, the chief tribe of Makkah, tried in many ways, including the use of force, to cause the Prophet Muhammad ﷺ to stray from his path, and to stop the message from spreading. So the Prophet was subjected to every kind of cruelty and insult, but he and his followers showed the utmost patience. When the persecution became very harsh and the Quraysh decided to kill the Prophet, he decided to leave Makkah. Under cover of darkness, the Prophet Muhammad ﷺ and Abu Bakr slipped away on camel-back, heading towards Madinah.

The Best Caller to God's Way

As the news of the Prophet Muhammad's arrival in Madinah spread throughout the city, the people climbed on the rooftops and scaled tall palm trees to glimpse him from afar. Spontaneously they sang to the beloved Prophet:

Tala'al-Badru 'alayna,
min thaniyyatil-Wada'
wajaba al-shukru 'alayna,
ma da'a lillahi da'

O the White Moon rose over us
From the Valley of Wada'
And we owe it to show gratefulness
Where the call is to Allah.

Ayyuha al-mab'uthu fina
ji'ta bi-al-amri al-muta'
Ji'ta sharrafta al-Madinah
Marhaban ya khayra da'

O you who were raised amongst us,
Coming with a word to be obeyed,
You have brought to this city nobleness.
Welcome! best caller to God's way.

In Madinah the Prophet was welcomed by the Ansars, who treated the immigrants as their brothers and sisters, and even shared their homes and possessions with them.

In Madinah, the Prophet founded the mosque, which is today known as the Mosque of the Prophet. He himself helped to build it. It became the centre of his activities, from which he would preach the message of Islam, sitting for hours on end in order to have the revelations written down and memorised by his companions.

The Prophet's kindness and merciful nature was unparalleled. Often, when he passed by a group of children, he would say, "Children are flowers of God," and pass his hand affectionately over their heads and sometimes even join in their innocent games. He had high regard for parents and specially honored them. Those, he believed, who served their parents well, were deserving of Paradise. A man once asked the Prophet, "Who rightfully deserves the best treatment from me?" "Your mother," said the Prophet. Then only after repeated questioning, did he say, "Your father." The Prophet gave great importance to family ties, good relations with neighbors and visiting the sick. He said that a visit to a sick person was like a visit to Allah. The Prophet's life was marked by simple living and sublime character, prayer and devotion, compassion and humility. After his death, people used to ask the Prophet's wife, Aishah, how he lived at home. "Like an ordinary man," she would answer.

"He would sweep the house, stitch his own clothes, mend his own sandals, water the camels, milk the goats, help the servants at their work, and eat his meal with them; and he would go to fetch what we needed from the market."

The Prophet Muhammad's Message of Peace

A great part of the Prophet's mission was to bring peace to the world. One way of doing so was to convince people that all men and women, although living in very different regions of the world, and seemingly different from one another in color, culture and language, etc., were in fact each other's blood brothers and sisters. The Prophet would preach to his followers: "You are all Adam's offspring and Adam was made of clay." And in his prayers to his Creator, he would say, "O Lord, all your servants are brothers."

The Prophet himself set an example of peaceful living with his great gentleness, kindness, humility, good humor and excellent common sense, and his great love for all people and even for animals. He never made others feel small, unwanted or embarrassed. He urged his followers to do likewise, to release slaves whenever possible, and give alms, especially to very poor people, orphans and prisoners—without any thought of reward.

He would tell people that "every religion has some special virtue, that of Islam being modesty." Without such a virtue, no community can have lasting peace.

He was of a high moral character, so that people might harm him, yet he would pray for them, returning good for evil. When others tried to provoke him, he would remain patient and serene. In setting this example, his real aim was to fashion souls

which were turned towards God, which found Allah so great that everything else seemed unimportant. This is expressed in one of the Prophet's sayings:

"Nine things the Lord has commanded me:
Fear of God in private and in public;
Justness, whether in anger or in calmness;
Moderation in both poverty and affluence;
That I should join hands with those who break away from me;
and give to those who deprive me;
and forgive those who wrong me;
and that my silence should be meditation;
and my words remembrance of God;
and my vision keen observation."
(Razin)